ON THE CASE!

K-9 UNITS

Madison Capitano

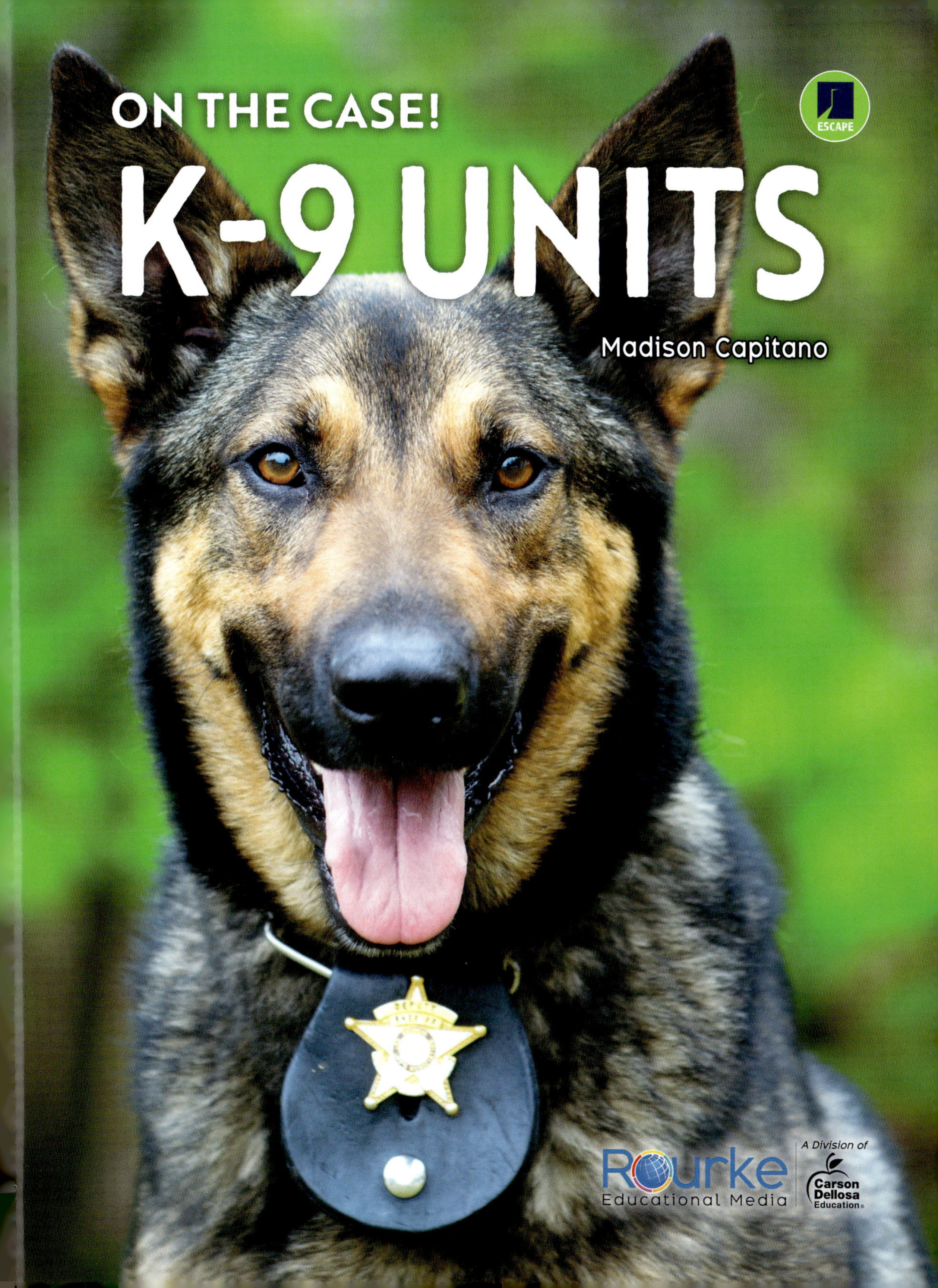

Rourke Educational Media
A Division of Carson Dellosa Education

ROURKE'S

SCHOOL to HOME

CONNECTIONS

BEFORE AND DURING READING ACTIVITIES

Before Reading: *Building Background Knowledge and Vocabulary*

Building background knowledge can help children process new information and build upon what they already know. Before reading a book, it is important to tap into what children already know about the topic. This will help them develop their vocabulary and increase their reading comprehension.

Questions and Activities to Build Background Knowledge:

1. Look at the front cover of the book and read the title. What do you think this book will be about?
2. What do you already know about this topic?
3. Take a book walk and skim the pages. Look at the table of contents, photographs, captions, and bold words. Did these text features give you any information or predictions about what you will read in this book?

Vocabulary: *Vocabulary Is Key to Reading Comprehension*

Use the following directions to prompt a conversation about each word.

- Read the vocabulary words.
- What comes to mind when you see each word?
- What do you think each word means?

Vocabulary Words:

- *bias*
- *cadaver*
- *canine*
- *detection*
- *handler*
- *informant*

During Reading: *Reading for Meaning and Understanding*

To achieve deep comprehension of a book, children are encouraged to use close reading strategies. During reading, it is important to have children stop and make connections. These connections result in deeper analysis and understanding of a book.

Close Reading a Text

During reading, have children stop and talk about the following:

- Any confusing parts
- Any unknown words
- Text to text, text to self, text to world connections
- The main idea in each chapter or heading

Encourage children to use context clues to determine the meaning of any unknown words. These strategies will help children learn to analyze the text more thoroughly as they read.

When you are finished reading this book, turn to the next-to-last page for **After Reading Questions** and an **Activity**.

TABLE OF CONTENTS

ON THE CASE

For hundreds of years, law enforcement officials have teamed up with dogs! Together, they tackle special cases. Each K-9 team is made up of a specially trained dog and its **handler**.

» **handler** (HAND-luhr): a person who trains or has charge of an animal

It takes a lot of work to be a part of a K-9 team. Both the handler and the **canine** partner must get certifications. Teams train for dealing with drug smuggling, missing persons cases, body retrieval searches, and more.

SOUNDS LIKE

Canine and *K-9* are homophones. Even though they are spelled differently, they sound the same. Crime fighting teams with dogs were called the K-9 Corps during World War II. The name stuck.

» **canine** (KAY-nine): a dog; of or related to dogs

A MYSTERIOUS BAG

An unmarked bag is found at the airport. What is inside? Could it be dangerous? Security makes a call. A K-9 unit is on the case!

When K-9 units come on the scene, they clear the area. Then, they investigate. **Detection** dogs smell for many things. They are trained to smell other animals, chemicals, explosives, and more.

» **detection** (di-TEKT-shuhn): discovering or determining something

When they smell something, detection dogs signal in different ways. This dog uses passive signaling by sitting down. Passive signaling is important when the dog smells something dangerous, such as bombs or chemicals. The mystery bag contained gunpowder!

CBP

A HIDDEN CAR

The police department gets a call from an **informant**. They say there is a car with drugs. But it is in a parking lot full of other cars. They do not know which one it is. A K-9 unit is on the case!

» **informant** (in-FOR-muhnt): a person who provides information, usually secret

Patrolling a parking lot is easy work for drug-sniffing dogs. They can smell drugs even when they are hidden. This dog is using active signaling to show that it smells drugs. Active signaling can mean digging or pawing at an area.

TRAINING TIME

Dogs sniff out drugs, bombs, and bodies because they want to play! One way to train detection dogs is to pair their favorite toy with certain smells. Once they find the smell, they know it's play time!

The signal from the detection dog lets the handler know to search the vehicle. This car had drugs hidden in the trunk!

ON THE NOSE

A dog's sense of smell is 40 times greater than a human's. What does that mean? If you put a teaspoon of sugar in a million gallons of water, a dog could *still* smell it!

1
2
OSS
CRIM

Detection dogs do make mistakes. Their sharp noses can smell traces of drugs instead of actual drugs. This can lead to unsuccessful searches.

Handler **bias** is also a problem. Dogs are more than just good noses. They can tell when their handlers are suspicious, scared, or upset.

» **bias** (BYE-uhs): a personal and sometimes unreasoned judgment against a particular group or person

A MISSING BODY

A missing persons case has the whole town on edge. The police know where to search. But it is a big forest. It's time to bring a K-9 unit on the case!

Detection dogs that look for dead bodies are also called **cadaver** dogs. Dead bodies have over 400 different smells. Cadaver dogs are trained to recognize them all.

» **cadaver** (kuh-DA-vur): a dead body

The police narrow the search down to one section of the forest. They send in cadaver dogs. With their help, the police find the body of a missing person even though it was buried over 12 feet (3.7 meters) underground!

THAT STINKS!

Some dogs can smell human remains that are over 30 years old.

K-9
K9

For over 100 years, heroic dog and human partners have been helping law enforcement make drug busts, catch criminals, and save lives. These dedicated teams spend years learning different ways to keep people safe. K-9 units are on the case!

MEMORY GAME

Look at the pictures. What do you remember reading on the pages where each image appeared?

INDEX

AFTER READING QUESTIONS

1. What is another name for detection dogs?
2. What is something that can trick a detection dog?
3. How much more sensitive is a dog's nose than a human's nose?
4. What are two things that an airport dog can be trained to smell?
5. What special strengths and abilities does each member bring to a K-9 team?

ACTIVITY

Imagine you are a K-9 handler. You and your dog must learn a new skill. What skill would you want to learn? Write why you choose that skill and which signal you would teach your dog to use.

ABOUT THE AUTHOR

Madison Capitano is a writer in Columbus, Ohio, who loves to watch mystery shows! She has a very sweet dog named Ivy, but she's not a police dog, she's a lap dog. Madison used to read books to her little brother and sister all the time. Now she loves to write books for other kids to enjoy.

www.rourkeeducationalmedia.com

PHOTO CREDITS: Cover: ©TK / TK; page 1: ©Rob Hainer / Shutterstock.com; page 5: ©Leonard Zhukovsky / Shutterstock.com; page 6: ©Heather Skau / Shutterstock.com; page 9: ©Jaromir Chalabala / Shutterstock.com; page 10: ©Monika Wisniewska / Shutterstock.com; page 13: ©James Tourtellotte / Flickr; page 15: ©KellyNelson / Shutterstock.com; page 16: ©Mike Hillingseter / Shutterstock.com; page 19: ©Mihajlo Maricic / iStockphoto; page 20: ©Victor Jiang / Shutterstock.com; page 23: ©kali9 / iStockphoto.com; page 24: ©Lillac / Shutterstock.com; page 24: ©Gerrit Bos / iStockphoto; page 27: ©NSC Photography / Shutterstock.com; page 28: ©John Roman Images / Shutterstock.com; caution tape: ©tcenitelkrasoti / Pixabay; magnifying glass: ©Pixaline / Pixabay

Edited by: Kim Thompson
Cover design by: Kathy Walsh
Interior design by: Sara Radka

Library of Congress PCN Data

K-9 Units / Madison Capitano
(On the Case!)
ISBN 978-1-73163-811-3 (hard cover)
ISBN 978-1-73163-888-5 (soft cover)
ISBN 978-1-73163-965-3 (e-Book)
ISBN 978-1-73164-042-0 (e-Pub)
Library of Congress Control Number: 2020930175

Rourke Educational Media
Printed in the United States of America
01-1662011937